EXTRAVAGANT
FAVOR

HOW TO WALK IN GOD'S
ABUNDANCE EVERY DAY

BILLY & BECKY EPPERHART

Published by Harrison House Publishers
Shippensburg, PA 17257

ISBN 13 TP: 978-1-6675-0281-6
ISBN 13 HC: 978-1-6675-0341-7
ISBN 13 eBook: 978-1-6675-0283-0

For Worldwide Distribution, Printed in the U.S.A.
1 2 3 4 5 6 7 8 / 27 26 25 24 23

DEDICATION

This book is dedicated to Andrew Wommack, one of the most authentic and humble people we have ever met. Aside from being one of the most prominent teachers and leaders in the Body of Christ, he is a friend and a shining example of God's favor in our lives.

ACKNOWLEDGMENTS

Mike and Carrie Pickett,
Vice Presidents of Charis Bible College

Andrew Wertz, Senior Vice President of Andrew
Wommack Ministries

The entire team at Andrew Wommack Ministries and
Charis Bible College

Hannah Echols Grieser, who helped us put this
teaching into the written word

CONTENTS

The Spirit of the Sovereign Lord is upon me, for the Lord has anointed me to bring good news to the poor. He has sent me to comfort the broken-hearted and to proclaim that captives will be released and prisoners will be freed. He has sent me to tell those who mourn that the time of the Lord's favor has come, and with it, the day of God's anger against their enemies.

ISAIAH 61:1-2 NLT

FOREWORD

by Lance Wallnau

You hold a treasure map to a life of supernatural Favor in your hands. Billy and Becky Epperhart's latest book, *Extravagant Favor,* is a rare find. It brings forth new insights on a subject seldom handled in the manner it is handled here. Favor is indeed a mysterious matter. It is a word in scripture that shows up in the life of Joseph, David, Esther, Daniel, Mary, and Jesus. Favor operates according to specific laws, releasing a cosmic power of divine attraction once set in motion. Like wealth, you cannot manufacture it, but you can live in a way that attracts it! Billy and Becky have lived this life of Favor and explain how you can attract and experience the same phenomena. One moment of divine Favor is more valuable than a lifetime of labor. It makes you a magnet to the people and resources you need to accomplish God's assignment. You see many aspects of the laws of Favor in the life of Philip, the evangelist in the book of Acts.

> *Now an angel of the Lord spoke to Philip, saying, "Arise and go toward the south along the road which goes down from Jerusalem to Gaza." This is desert. So he arose and went. And behold, a man of Ethiopia, a eunuch of great authority under Candace, the queen of the Ethiopians, who had charge of all her treasury, and had come to Jerusalem to worship, was returning. And sitting in his chariot, he was reading Isaiah the prophet. Then the Spirit said to Philip, "Go near and overtake this chariot." So Philip ran to him, and heard him reading the prophet Isaiah, and said, "Do*

you understand what you are reading?" (Acts 8:26-30 NKJV).

Philip led that treasurer to the Lord, but there is a unique sequence in what took place: first, he heard God give him a direction, and he obeyed. Philip was not told about the treasurer; he was told about the direction. Second, a divine appointment occurred when he got to the place God sent him. It was then that the Spirit further instructed him to join the chariot. Since the chariot was in motion, Philip had to run to catch up on his divine appointment. It always struck me that God didn't make it easy for Phillip—he still had to hustle to the chariot! When God wanted Phillip to minister to that high-ranking treasurer, He did not plop him into the man's chariot. Instead, Philip was placed in proximity and urged to run.

In a way, that sequence applies to you. God has given you this book. Maybe this is a divine appointment for you. Perhaps an angel set this up. You now have keys to the force of Favor in proximity to you. Don't miss your *Extravagant Favor* chariot! I encourage you to run with these ideas. I've seen great wealth and influence multiply in the Epperhart's lives. The reason? You can find the secret in their book. They paid the price to build the consistency and character required to handle the divine force of Favor. These ideas work!

Whether you're a business owner, a student, a parent, or anyone seeking to walk in God's Favor, this book offers practical wisdom and inspiration. You hold a treasure map in your hand. Enjoy the journey.

Dr. Lance Wallnau
The Lance Learning Group
Dallas, Texas

WALKING WITH GOD

Thousands of years ago, there lived a man who never died.

When he was born, the earth was still young. Yet humanity was already spiraling out of control. Ancient records reveal that creation was altogether evil.[1] However, this man shone as a diamond in the rough. His name was Enoch, which means dedicated, and his only known characteristic is that he walked with God.

Genesis 5:23-24 (NLT) says, *"Enoch lived 365 years, walking in close fellowship with God. Then one day he disappeared, because God took him."*

Enoch walked so closely with God that he evaded death and was transported straight to heaven. This brief story stirs a deep curiosity within me—what does it mean to walk with God?

The Hebrew word for "walk" is *hālak*.[2] Literally it means to walk, come, depart, proceed, move, or go away. Figuratively, *hālak* means much more than that. It's used throughout the Old Testament to describe a way of life. How you *hālak* determines your direction, literally and spiritually. It's the difference between living from God's favor or scraping by in your own strength.

Consider Psalm 84:11 (ESV): *"For the Lord is a sun and shield; the Lord bestows favor and honor. No good thing does he withhold to those who walk* [hālak] *uprightly."*

Walking is slow. It's consistent. It's not dramatic. Yet it yields results. When you walk with God, you will experience His favor. You may not get raptured into heaven like Enoch, but you will begin to see God work in the daily details of your life, from your family to your finances.

When we talk about walking in God's favor, we mean accepting His grace in every area of life. In fact, the Bible often uses the words "favor" and "grace" interchangeably. Let's look at two verses:

- ► 2 Corinthians 9:8 (ESV) says, *"And God is able to make all grace abound to you, so that having all sufficiency in all things at all times, you may abound in every good work."*
- ► Luke 1:30 (ESV) says, *"And the angel said to her, 'Do not be afraid, Mary, for you have found favor with God.'"*

In both instances (as well as 150+ other times in the New Testament), the word *charis* is used.[3] It translates to that which affords joy, pleasure, delight, sweetness, charm, loveliness, good will, lovingkindness, and favor. So favor is an inextricable part of God's grace. You can't have one without the other.

We are never entitled to grace. It is the unmerited, or undeserved, favor of God. And it's *extravagant*. All we have to do is walk with God, and then He lavishes grace that we do not deserve. This extravagance extends from earthly blessings to eternal life!

As Ephesians 2:8-9 (ESV) says, *"For by grace you have been saved through faith. And this is not your own doing; it is the gift of God, not a result of works, so that no one may boast."* You can't earn favor, but you can ignore it. Like any gift, you can choose to open it or not. Perhaps you resemble a kid halfway into January. You received your new gifts enthusiastically on Christmas Day and played with them until New Year's. However, as time trickled on, the presents were left under your bed to collect dust.

So how do we unwrap and consistently use the gifts God has prepared for us? *We open our hands and ask.* It's as simple as that. However, it's not easy. To receive, you must let go of what you are holding.

Favor Follows Surrender

People get excited about favor, but they run away from surrender. Nonetheless, favor flows from the foundation of surrender. From the moment a child is born, God's favor follows that child. When the child responds by accepting God as Lord and Savior, favor surrounds the youngster like a shield, as they become engulfed in grace so strong that it conquers death and offers eternity, for *"whoever believes in Him should not perish but have everlasting life"* (John 3:16 NKJV).

Accepting Jesus as your Lord and Savior is the first form of surrender that activates God's favor in your life. Jesus did not beat around the bush about the degree of sacrifice required to follow Him. He encouraged His disciples to count the cost when He said, *"For which of you, desiring to build a tower, does not first sit down and count the cost, whether he has enough to complete it?"* Jesus concluded, *"So therefore, any one of you who does not renounce all that he has cannot be my disciple"* (Luke 14:28,33 ESV).

So, a moment of surrender will grant you eternal life. However, if you want to follow Jesus and walk in God's favor continuously, surrender must become a daily practice. Jesus addresses the need for daily surrender in the Sermon on the Mount by acknowledging the human tendency to worry about food, clothing, and material provision. He promises, *"Seek first the kingdom of God and His righteousness, and all these things shall be added to you"* (Matt. 6:33 NKJV).

God won't give you a blessing your character can't handle. Favor is attracted to your life when you pursue kingdom priorities. Our motives get distorted as soon as we pursue our plans and purposes. If we pursue money, we become greedy. If we pursue influence, we become prideful. If we pursue opportunities, we become controlling. However, if we pursue the kingdom of God, everything will be added. It's the principle of giving and receiving. Favor is unlocked when we give our time, talents, and treasure to further the kingdom of heaven on earth.

Get Off the Couch and Walk

As your understanding of the kingdom gets deeper, your perspective becomes clearer. It has taken decades to focus my perspective. When I was younger, I had little to no concept of the kingdom. I worked as a pastor for twenty-eight years and loved the Lord. Our church's main priority was getting people saved, which is paramount. However, I didn't have a great picture of how the gospel could inform the practical parts of my life, such as my job and finances. Those things were considered secular in that day and age, and the church was considered sacred. Consequently, pastors were discouraged from having streams of income other than their church salary.

So as someone with an entrepreneurial and financial bent, I kept my business and investment activities separate from my faith. Because of shame, I didn't let the kingdom infuse those areas of my life. In fact, I was eager to reach financial freedom so that my family's livelihood wouldn't have to depend on the church. By the time I was 48, I had replaced all my earned income with passive income.

I became financially free for entirely selfish reasons. I was afraid of not having enough, so I did not think about how I could serve God with my money. Though God's grace was on my life as a believer, I often didn't choose to walk in His favor. In several instances, I kicked down doors rather than waiting for God's favor to open them. I ran at my own speed rather than submitting to the pace of grace.

During the first two years of my retirement, I pretty much did whatever I wanted to do. It didn't take long for my wife to have a little talk with me. She lovingly said, "Billy, if you don't get off the couch, I'm going to kill you." I saluted her and realized she was right. If I stayed on the couch, I was going to die young.

As Albert Einstein said, "Once you stop learning, you start dying." I didn't reach financial freedom so that I could play golf every day. If I wanted to fulfill God's will for my life, I had to give a new level of surrender. I asked God what He wanted to do with my newfound time and money. Then, He led me on an adventure.

The phrase "the gospel of the kingdom" began to stand out to me in scripture. I began to wonder what Jesus meant when He said, *"Repent, for the kingdom of heaven is at hand"* (Matt. 4:17 NKJV) and *"Your kingdom come, Your will be done, on earth as it is in heaven"* (Matt. 6:10 NKJV).

During that time, I started hearing about a mission strategy called the Seven Mountains. The concept was originally developed in the 1970's and 80's by Bill Bright, the founder of Campus Crusade for Christ, as "seven world kingdoms" or "seven spheres," and by Loren Cunningham, the founder of Youth with a Mission, as "seven mind-molders" of culture. Lance Wallnau later catalyzed the concept to a new generation of believers as the "Seven Mountains." In the Bible, mountains are a symbol of world kingdoms. The Bible makes an interesting description of the end of this age: *"Now it shall come to pass in the latter days that the mountain of the Lord's house shall be established on the top of the mountains, and shall be exalted above the hills; and all nations shall flow to it."* (Isaiah 2:2)

These mountains of cultural influence are: religion, family, education, government, arts & media, science, and business. Favor is a major factor in the journey to the top of the mountains. The goal for the Body of Christ is to glorify God in every nation by penetrating and reforming every area of culture with Kingdom principles.

We were sitting on the back row at a conference when he leaned over and said, "You know, we have been really good at preaching the gospel of salvation, but we haven't been good at preaching the gospel of the kingdom."

At that moment, the pieces began to fit together. The seven mountains are integral to the gospel of the kingdom. God wants to establish His will on earth through every sphere of society. So that meant God had a divine purpose for my love of business and finance. My passion could give others a taste of the kingdom of God. Goodbye shame, and hello purpose!

The same goes for you. Your daily work matters. What particular grace has God put on your life? What is your sphere of influence? When you "seek first the kingdom," God will lead you. His purposes for you are attracted, not pursued.

Once I reached a new level of surrender, greater doors opened. My plans didn't suffocate what God wanted to do in my life. I met people who helped me become the CEO of Andrew Wommack Ministries and Charis Bible College. God gave us the idea for our nonprofits, WealthBuilders and Tricord Global. I cannot begin to scratch the surface of everything God has done in one book.

The Bible says that God shows no favoritism (see Acts 10:34 NLT). What He does for one, He will do for another. If you apply the tools in this book, *Extravagant Favor,* God's favor will define your story. There are people you've never met, experiences you've never had, and opportunities you've never imagined in store for your future.

This book includes seven principles Becky and I have learned about recognizing and walking in God's abundant favor. It is written in my (Billy's) voice for clarity, but every concept flows directly from the lessons we've learned corporately through the Word of God—and a lot of trial and error! We wrote this book together so that you don't have to make the same mistakes we did. If you implement these principles, your life and the lives of those around you will never be the same.

CHAPTER 1

FAVOR IS ATTRACTED TO A SPIRIT OF PREPARATION

When you start something new, you probably won't be good at it.

For example, if you want to learn a new language, you won't be able to hold a conversation in the beginning. If you want to start painting, your work may look like a first-grader's art project at first. And if you want to build wealth, there will probably be a time when your income is low and your debt is high. Nevertheless, if you prepare, you will be a multilingual speaker, capable artist, or wise investor one day.

Your level of preparation reveals your belief in God's future favor.

Christians often misunderstand faith as a passive act. On the contrary, God usually asks us to prepare for the blessing before it comes. Just as a beginner athlete's commitment to practice indicates faith in their future success, our level of preparation reveals our belief in God's future favor.

God's favor is attracted to a spirit of preparation. When you prepare, you partner with God by activating your belief in an unseen result. One of my favorite stories about preparation in the Bible is about a young man named Jehoiachin. Instead of letting a difficult situation crush him, he used it as an opportunity to prepare.

Preparation in Prison

Jehoiachin became the king of Judah when he was 18 years old. The Bible says he *"did evil in the sight of the Lord"* during his reign (2 Kings 24:8 NKJV). After three months into his kingship, the officials of the Babylonian king Nebuchadnezzar laid siege to Jerusalem and took Jehoiachin as a prisoner.

I don't know what kind of evil Jehoiachin did, but I imagine it would be hard to lead a nation at age 18. In consequence, Jehoiachin spent some time in prison. After the Babylonians wreaked havoc on Judah for thirty-seven years, a new king replaced Nebuchadnezzar. He released Jehoiachin from prison and extravagantly blessed him:

> ...in the first year of his reign, [he] showed favor to Jehoiachin king of Judah and brought him out of prison. He spoke kindly to him and gave him a throne above the thrones of the kings who were [captives] with him in Babylon. Jehoiachin changed his prison clothes, and he dined regularly at the king's table all the days of his life. And his allowance, a regular allowance was given to him by the king of Babylon, a daily portion [according to his needs] until the day of his death, all the days of his life (Jeremiah 52:31-34 AMP).

The new king showed Jehoiachin favor. He dined at the king's table every day, which I imagine was pretty good eating. He received a daily allowance, too. When I read this passage, I wondered, *What made Jehoiachin so special?* I prayed, "God, You make it clear throughout the Scriptures that You don't show favoritism. So why would You show favor to Jehoiachin and not the other kings? Why was he unique?"

After praying, I studied the meaning of Jehoiachin's name and made a discovery. According to Hitchcock's Bible Names Dictionary, the name Jehoiachin means preparation.[4] In Jehoiachin's time, it was common to name people prophetically or to rename them based on how they lived. So it's safe to assume that Jehoiachin prepared. He didn't waste those thirty-seven years in prison. I believe he was obedient to what God told him to do in captivity, whether teaching, preaching, or praying. While he was a prisoner, Jehoiachin prepared to be a king. The Lord watched him grow and mature, and when the timing was right, he reached down and elevated him above the rest.

Favor is attracted to people who never stop believing that God's best is possible. He will use everything—the good, the bad, and the ugly—and turn it around for your good. When you prepare in faith, God will reward you.

Luck Versus Favor

Did you know that nearly one-third of lottery winners go bankrupt within a few years of claiming their prize?[5] Most lottery winners never learn how to manage large amounts of money. Regardless of how much money you make, you will lose everything that comes to you if you don't learn how to steward it.

So what does the lottery have to do with favor?

Well, many people think favor is similar to winning the lottery. They assume favor comes by luck or chance. However, you have more agency than that. Remember, favor is attracted to a spirit of preparation. We don't need our *luck* to change. *We* need to change.

Jesus illustrated the power of preparation in a story referred to as the Parable of the Talents. You can read the entire parable in Matthew 25:14-30.

> *Jesus said, "For it [the kingdom of heaven] will be like a man going on a journey, who called his servants and entrusted to them his property. To one he gave five talents, to another two, to another one, to each according to his ability. Then he went away"* (Matthew 25:14-15 ESV).

Did you catch that? The master awards each servant with an amount of money *according to their abilities.* He observed the capabilities of each servant and awarded the most capable person with the most money. The servant who received five talents walked in a spirit of preparation before the master's departure. He cultivated the ability to carry more responsibility.

On the contrary, I think the master was giving the servant with one talent a chance. He knew that servant was a novice, but he gave him a shot to see what kind of attitude and heart posture he had. As the parable will show us, that servant squanders his opportunity.

> **Cultivate the ability to carry more responsibility.**

Money Is Attracted, Not Pursued

The scripture continues, *"After a long absence, the master of those three servants came back and settled up with them. The one given five thousand dollars showed him how he had doubled his investment. 'His master commended him: "Good work! You did your job well. From now on be my partner""*(Matt. 25:19-21 MSG). The servant with two talents also doubled his investment and received congratulations.

However, the servant with one talent did not fulfill his assignment. He wasn't profitable with his talent. Rather than multiplying the money, he hid it and did not prepare for his boss's return. The master was furious. He said:

That's a terrible way to live! It's criminal to live cautiously like that! If you knew I was after the best, why did you do less than the least? The least you could have done would have been to invest the sum with the bankers, where at least I would have gotten a little interest (Matthew 25:26-27 MSG).

Then the master does something really interesting. He takes the talent from the unfaithful servant and gives it to the servant with ten talents. He says, *"Take the thousand and give it to the one who risked the most. And get rid of this 'play-it-safe' who won't go out on a limb. Throw him out into utter darkness"* (Matt. 25:28-30 MSG). The English Standard Version of the Bible puts Matthew 25:29 this way: *"For to everyone who has will more be given, and he will have an abundance. But from the one who has not, even what he has will be taken away."* The servant with ten talents operated in a spirit of preparation. As a result, additional favor was added to the already-doubled investment. Through this parable, Jesus charged His disciples to steward their current assignment.

As you multiply what God has put in your hand, He will give you more when the time is right. When it comes to your finances, money is attracted, not pursued. In other words, success doesn't come by restlessly seeking out the next opportunity. It comes through God's favor. Rather than focusing on what we don't have, the Bible encourages us to maximize the current opportunities under our stewardship. Then He will increase and call us to more responsibility.

**Maximize your
current opportunities.**

First and foremost, good stewardship requires a posture of partnership with God. Good stewards recognize that they have been entrusted with resources for a temporary period. As the psalmist writes in Psalm 24:1 (NLT), *"The earth is the Lord's, and everything in it."* Everything we have belongs to God. Yet when we give our God-given resources back to Him, He gives back to us with added increase! Generously giving is a primary way to attract money to your life.

The apostle Paul describes this in 2 Corinthians 9:6-8 (NLT). He writes:

> *Remember this—a farmer who plants only a few seeds will get a small crop. But the one who plants generously will get a generous crop. You must each decide in your heart how much to give. And don't give reluctantly or in response to pressure. "For God loves a person who gives cheerfully." And God will generously provide all you need. Then you will always have everything you need and plenty left over to share with others.*

Our money is like a seed. We can use it to grow resources for the kingdom and watch as God multiplies our impact and return on investment. Or we can eat our seed by spending it on things that lose their value. When we do this, we miss out on the miraculous multiplication God intended.

Generous people attract resources because giving creates a character that can carry more. God will give you resources to meet your needs and empower you to share with others.

The Parable of the Talents shows us that good stewardship isn't just about giving generously. It also requires multiplication. We may only see a seed, but God sees generations of an orchard that can feed thousands. Money is attracted to your life when you gain knowledge, understanding, and wisdom (in that order) about how to manage it well.

Too often, we dissociate the idea of having wisdom from the process of obtaining knowledge. Financial wisdom won't just plop into your brain. You must gain knowledge through things like books, schooling, podcasts, and trusted mentors. Then you must get in the game to apply the knowledge you've learned. That's how understanding develops. After you repeat the process several times, you will gain wisdom.

You can't bypass this system if you want to steward large amounts of resources for the kingdom of God. Remember, the master in the Parable of the Talents gave each servant an amount according to their ability. Becoming a five-talent person requires submitting to the learning process.

That's why Proverbs 24:3-4 (AMP) says, *"Through [skillful and godly] wisdom a house [a life, a home, a family] is built, and by understanding it is established [on a sound and good foundation], and by knowledge its rooms are filled with all precious and pleasant riches."* All three—knowledge, understanding, and wisdom—are necessary components for a successful enterprise. So the next chapter discusses how you can be faithful through every stage of the journey.

ACTIVATE: Don't Scale Too Quickly

It's important to steward what we have before we try to acquire more. In business terms, this is called scaling too quickly. For instance, you don't want to hire employees you don't have the capacity to pay, and you don't want to undertake responsibilities you don't have the employees to fulfill. The same paradigm applies to wisely stewarding our finances and careers.

For example, you shouldn't buy a television on credit if you don't have the money to pay for it. You shouldn't leave a job before you fulfill the assignment God has given you there. It is wasteful to acquire more before we properly steward what we have. Inevitably, things will slip through the cracks, and we won't fulfill God's will for us in that space. It takes discipline to maximize current opportunity when all you want to do is escape to the next thing. If you trust God to add the increase rather than moving forward in your own strength, you will be rewarded.

CHAPTER 2

FAVOR FOLLOWS FAITHFULNESS

Preparation starts with the little things.

People often want to step into the full measure of their destiny at a young age. That would be like giving a seven-year-old the keys to the family car. The child wouldn't know what to do with them! When Becky and I were in college, we accepted a ministry internship. At the time, we were ready to take on the world. However, once we started the internship, it was totally different from what we expected. Becky had to arrive at five o'clock in the morning to work as a cook. She also pulled challenging shifts in the children's daycare area of the ministry.

On the other hand, my first task was to clean buses. It took me five days to scrub more than twenty vehicles. When Friday afternoon came along, I proudly said, "I washed all the buses!" The internship director said, "Good job! Now I want you to go back and clean the inside of each bus." I had a pretty good attitude the first go-around, but while working on the insides, I was grumbling up a storm. However, the Lord used that internship to teach me the value of faithfulness.

A Foundation of Faithfulness

Luke 16:10 (AMP) says, *"He who is faithful in a very little thing is faithful in much; and he who is dishonest in a very little thing is dishonest and in much."*

The skills we cultivate through being faithful with small things are the same skills we need to be faithful with large things. Faithfulness is a process. We don't automatically understand how to be faithful when we become a Christian. If we did, God would go ahead and trust us with large things right off the bat.

Faithfulness is a process.

So, you must learn how to be faithful in the little things. What are the little things? Your job. Your relationships. Your finances. Your spiritual life. Your talents. The little things are what you currently have in your hands. They are the responsibilities and joys you have been entrusted with today. Like the Parable of the Talents teaches, more will be added when you steward those things well. The increase that God provides is favor.

If you've ever played golf, you know that putting requires more than hitting the ball in a straight direction. To sink the shot, you must be mindful of the terrain and other environmental factors. If there is a hill or wind, you may have to putt the ball away from the hole. Then the ball will curve around the obstacle and land in the cup.

When it comes to being faithful in the small things, it may feel like you're putting away from the hole at first. For instance, say that your dream is to be an author, but you're currently working at a coffee shop. If you're faithful and do the job to the best of your ability, favor will follow. Perhaps you've progressed to the point where you're managing someone else's manuscript. Rather than complaining that you're not writing your own books yet, be faithful and soak up the lessons God has for you in this season. God's favor will follow and promote you at the right time.

As Psalm 75:6-7 (KJV) says, *"For promotion cometh neither from the east, nor from the west, nor from the south. But God is the judge: he putteth down one, and setteth up another."* Everything God wants to do in your life will be built upon the foundation of faithfulness. God often teaches us how to be faithful through serving someone else.

Serve Another Person's Vision

> *Therefore if you have not been faithful in the use of earthly wealth, who will entrust the true riches to you? And if you have not been faithful in the use of that [earthly wealth] which belongs*

*to another [whether God or man, and of which
you are a trustee], who will give you that which
is your own?* (Luke 16:11-12 AMP)

According to Jesus, a key component of faith-fulness is serving others. We never graduate from serving. Jesus, the Lord of the universe, washed the disciples' feet! As you continue to grow, there will always be an opportunity to serve someone else's vision. This applies to everyone, whether you're a CEO or a college student. In fact, as the CEO of Andrew Wommack Ministries and Charis Bible College, I serve the vision of Andrew and Jamie Wommack. I also ensure the employees in my down-line (all 1,200+ of them) have everything they need to fulfill the vision of the ministry.

Favor follows faithful service.

There's a spiritual principle at work here. It's true for Christians who work in churches and Christians who work in the marketplace. *Favor follows faith-ful service.* When you serve, you realize that your purpose is bigger than you. Service purifies self-ish ambition—and we all have some. When we are faithful in serving another person's vision, we develop the kind of character that can be faithful in serving God's vision for our lives. However, faithful service requires patience.

Patience

In today's day and age, we are addicted to instant gratification. The phone in my pocket is a constant reminder of that. Every morning, I pop my breakfast into the microwave. With the push of a button, ready-to-eat oatmeal appears. When I was younger, it took me much longer to cook the same meal in a skillet.

Nobody likes to talk about patience. We want what we want when we want it. Has God ever given you a promise, only to have you wait for years until it's fulfilled? Maybe you're still waiting. As hard as it is to wait, God doesn't dangle carrots. When He makes a promise, it will come to pass.

A pastor I know defines patience as "faith enduring over a long period of time." One of the Bible's most renowned heroes knew a lot about this kind of patience, and like you and me, he made a few fumbles in the waiting process. Genesis 12:2-3 (AMPC) recounts God's promises to Abram:

> *And I will make of you a great nation, and I will bless you [with abundant increase of favors] and make your name famous and distinguished, and you will be a blessing [dispensing good to others]. And I will bless those who bless you [who confer prosperity or happiness upon you] and curse him who curses or uses insolent language toward you; in you will all the families and kindred of the earth be blessed [and by you they will bless themselves].*

God promised to show His favor to Abram and his family. However, Abram was going to have to be patient for that favor. In fact, Abram and his wife, Sarai would wait twenty-five years for the birth of their son, Isaac.[6] God promised to bless the earth through Abram's family (before he had kids). Months pass, and then years. What would you do if you were in Abram's shoes? Perhaps you would wonder if God's promises were a metaphor—a figure of speech. Maybe you'd forget your calling. Or, like Abram and Sarai, you might be tempted to take matters into your own hands.

"And Sarai said to Abram, 'Behold now, the Lord has prevented me from having children…'" (Gen. 16:2 ESV). That's red flag number one. Instead of being patient with God's timing, Sarai gave up. She convinced herself that God removed the very favor He promised to give her. She continues, *"Go in to my servant; it may be that I shall obtain children by her."*

Abram listens to Sarai, and her servant Hagar has a son, Ishmael. However, God doesn't establish His covenant with Ishmael. As God promised, the covenant would come through Abram's descendants. If you don't have patience, you will settle for less than God's best.

As Hebrews 6:12 (NKJV) says, we inherit the promises of God *"through faith and patience."* The preparation part is faith, and the waiting is patience. James 1:4 (NKJV) encourages, *"But let patience have its perfect work, that you may be perfect and complete, lacking nothing."* This verse describes patience as a developmental process. We don't come out of the womb knowing how to be patient. However, as the fruit of the Spirit ripens in you, patience will have its perfect work.

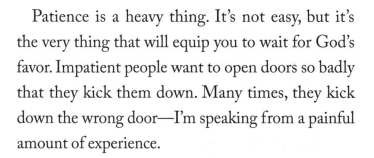

You inherit the promises of God through faith and patience.

Patience is a heavy thing. It's not easy, but it's the very thing that will equip you to wait for God's favor. Impatient people want to open doors so badly that they kick them down. Many times, they kick down the wrong door—I'm speaking from a painful amount of experience.

On the contrary, when you have faith that endures, God's favor will open the right doors and close the wrong doors. That's the difference between self-promotion and stewardship. When you have patience, you can effectively steward what the Lord has entrusted to you. Without it, you will try to promote yourself when God still has lessons for you in your current situation.

When you prefer your own timing, you won't get the whole enchilada of what God has planned for you. Instead, you settle for part of the plate. Hebrews 10:36 (AMPC) says, *"For you have need of steadfast patience and endurance, so that you may perform and fully accomplish the will of God, and thus receive and carry away [and enjoy to the full] what is promised."*

It takes patience to walk in the will of God. That's because God's will is bigger than you. It involves other people and organizations, so the timing must be orchestrated beyond you and your schedule. The next chapter dives into how God's favor is released through other people and divine timing.

ACTIVATE: Be Consistent

What are some areas in your life where you struggle to be patient? You can identify them by taking stock of the times you're the most tempted to escape into a different reality. When I was younger, waiting for God to move in my investments and business tested my patience. My tendency was to lead the charge and step out or into a venture before I got a thumbs-up from God. Here's a nugget—the things that are the most difficult for you to be patient in are usually tied to your unique purpose in life. I had to learn how to lean on God in financial matters because I would later teach others how to do the same. God redeems our broken areas and gives us strength in those weaknesses for His glory.

When you want to escape, choose consistency instead. Consistency is a cardinal rule of investing. If you consistently invest in the real estate or stock market and don't pull out when times are hard, over time your money will compound. This truth translates to every area of life.

If you struggle with faithfulness, God's favor will help you strengthen that spiritual muscle. First John 4:19 (NKJV) says, *"We love Him because He first loved us."* Well, the same rings true for every fruit of the Spirit—we are faithful because He was first faithful. Ask God to reveal His faithfulness to you and let that revelation energize and sustain all your pursuits.

CHAPTER 3

FAVOR IS RELEASED THROUGH A SPIRIT OF ASSOCIATION

Sociologists have found that you will influence over 10,000 people in your lifetime.[7] On the other hand, you will be impacted by thousands of people, too. For better and for worse, each one of us is a part of multiple systems and spheres of influence. It's like a set of dominoes—we move because someone else moves, and we move someone else because we have been moved.

Despite this reality, it is easy to fixate on our individual purpose and destiny. However, the truth is that our calling is corporate. As the Body of Christ, our calling *"to make disciples of all nations"* would be impossible alone! (See Matthew 28:19.)

Before He went to the cross, Jesus prayed, "...*that they may be one even as we are one, I in them and you in me, that they may become perfectly one, so that the world may know that you sent me and loved them even as you loved me*" (John 17:22-23 ESV). Jesus was talking about us! The world will experience God through the witness of our relationships.

 Relationships pave the path to God's plans and purposes for your life.

God releases favor through a spirit of association. In other words, relationships pave the path to God's plans and purposes for your life. The Bible recounts that God will move history for the sake of His people. Isaiah 43:4-6 (NKJV) reveals God's plan to gather people together:

> *Since you were precious in My sight, you have been honored, and I have loved you; therefore I will give men for you, and people for your life. Fear not, for I am with you; I will bring your descendants from the east, and gather you from*

the west; I will say to the north, "Give them
up!" And to the south, "Do not keep them back!"
Bring My sons from afar, and My daughters
from the ends of the earth.

God will bring the right people into your life at the right time. I refer to the right people as divine connections and the right times as *kairos* moments. Becky and I pray for divine connections from the Lord every morning. Our prayer goes something like this: "Father, thank You that You have people for our lives. We believe there are people in the north. We believe there are people in the south. We believe there are people in the east. We believe there are people in the west. Lord, we speak to the north, we speak to the west, we speak to the east, we speak to the south, and we command it to give up the people who belong in our lives."

Then as we come across people throughout our day, we believe that God has divine appointments that could lead to divine connections. You will be a divine connection for others, too. Some relationships, such as your spouse and family, will stay with you your whole life. Others will only be with you for a season.

A divine connection can even be a matter of life and death. Two weeks before my grandson was born, a French doctor who was the foremost expert in the infant heart defect TGA briefly moved to Denver. Well, this particular grandson (we have four) happened to be born with TGA. By God's grace, this doctor saved my grandson, and shortly after, he moved back to France. God may use some divine connections for a moment—and that moment can change the course of history.

Kairos Moments

A small encounter with a divine connection can affect you in a big way. I first learned this from a stranger with a yellow sticky note. I was speaking at a conference, and right before I walked to the stage, I placed my iPad on my seat. When I returned, there was an itty-bitty sticky note on the screen with "Don't go back" scrawled on it.

At the time, Becky and I were going through one of the most significant transitions of our lives. In the midst of the change, we were considering returning to old responsibilities. The stranger's timely encouragement gave us the nudge we needed to stick to our season. I'm so glad we did because God had a purpose for our transition. As Proverbs 15:23 (ESV) says, *"To make an apt answer is a joy to a man, and a word in season, how good it is!"*

> **Walking in God's favor means submitting to His timeline, even when you don't understand it.**

An integral part of walking in God's favor is submitting to His timeline even when we don't understand it. Think about it: if your destiny depends on divine connections, the timing of events in your life must make sense for another group of people, too. You may feel like you've been waiting forever when the delay is actually representative of God's favor. He orchestrates people and opportunities at the opportune, or *kairos*, moment.

The ancient Greeks had two words for time—chronos and kairos. Chronos refers to measurable, quantitative time. In other words, chronos is clock time. It's chronological and can be measured in hours, days, weeks, months…you get the picture. On the other hand, kairos time is qualitative. It measures moments. And not just any moment—an opportune, or favorable, moment.[8]

In the Bible, *kairos* is used to describe the appointed time for the purposes of God, such as when Jesus says, *"The time is fulfilled, and the kingdom of God is at hand. Repent, and believe in the gospel"* (Mark 1:15 NKJV).

Kairos time explains why God can accomplish something in a few months when it would take years for humans to complete the same task. A *kairos* moment is a critical juncture that God aligns for a particular purpose. It happens whenever God's plans disrupt your plans.

The Holy Spirit will help you discern *kairos* time. Jesus says in John 16:13 (ESV), *"When the Spirit of truth comes, he will guide you into all the truth, for he will not speak on his own authority, but wherever he hears he will speak, and he will declare to you the things that are to come."* Knowing that the Holy Spirit will lead us into all truth is an encouragement to pray with confidence!

Your Treasure Chest

Did you know that God dreams over you? Sometimes we have a dream and ask God to bless it. Other times, God has a dream and puts it into the hearts of His people. Then His favor draws them together. When you start running and gunning with the vision God has put into your heart, you will begin meeting people who are moving toward the same goal.

Divine connections and *kairos* moments act as spiritual breadcrumbs that lead you toward the dreams God has for your life. This could materialize in all sorts of ways. Maybe a friend invites you to his or her church. Perhaps someone gives you a job opportunity or becomes a vital business partnership.

Envision a treasure chest. Inside that treasure chest are people you've never met and experiences you've never had. Rather than jewels and gold, it's filled to the brim with God's dreams for your life. God has already prepared the treasure chest. All you have to do is open the lid. However, many people close the lid due to pain and disappointment instead. Past hurt can result in lost hope. You can choose to let the grace of God refine your pain so that it doesn't define your future.

The Bible says that God shows no partiality (see Acts 10:34 ESV). As mentioned previously, what He does for one, He will do for another. I have seen God's favor overflow through divine connections and *kairos* moments in my life. So I know your treasure chest is locked and loaded, too. Unfortunately, many people never walk in the blessings of God—not because they don't want to, but because they don't notice them.

Malachi 3:10 (NKJV) provides some guidance on how to activate your spiritual eyes to recognize divine connections and *kairos* moments:

> *"Bring all the tithes into the storehouse, that there may be food in My house, and try Me now in this," says the Lord of hosts, "If I will not open for you the windows of heaven and pour out for you such blessing that there will not be room enough to receive it."*

The purpose of a window is to help you see more. It expands your perspective. When we partner with God through our tithes and offerings, the windows of heaven open wide. When you surrender your time, talent, and treasure to further the kingdom of heaven, God will give you revelation and insight on where to access an abundance of resources.

When 30 Become 30,000

Once you have a revelation of your treasure chest, favor starts to become an attitude. When you are confident that God has unique appointments, people, and opportunities for you every day, you can walk in a spirit of association. While favor anchors you to the present, it also directs your sights toward the abundance of heaven. Even in seasons of scarcity, you know that there are more opportunities for increase inside your treasure chest. The abundance has your name on it, but the *kairos* moment for its release hasn't come yet.

Favor anchors you to the present and directs your sights toward the abundance of heaven.

One divine connection proved this principle to us. I used to be a pastor in a relatively small church. On Wednesday nights, I'd preach to about thirty adults.

At times it was discouraging because God gave us a vision for a much larger congregation.

At that church we turned some of our teachings into cassette tapes and gave them away in visitor packets. One day as I was getting the oil changed in my red Ford Explorer, my phone rang. Back then, I had a giant cell phone with no caller ID. I only gave my phone number to my wife and secretary, so I was curious. If someone had given my number to this guy, it must have been important. I answered the phone.

"Is this Pastor Billy Epperhart?"

"It is. How may I help you?"

He replied, "I have a cassette tape of yours. As a matter of fact, I have two cassette tapes of yours, and I've given them a listen. We want to publish these."

Puzzled, I asked, "Uh, how does that work?"

"Just send me two sermon tapes every month. We'll take a listen, clean out personal details related to the church, and duplicate it," he explained.

"How many tapes do you send out?"

"Well, we send out 30,000 tapes a week. You would get paid royalties per tape. Just send us the message, we produce everything, and then we will send you money per tape sold."

"So you send out 30,000 tapes, and you'll pay me a royalty per each tape sold?" I asked, heavily intrigued at this point.

"Yes! We'll send you a check once a month on the royalties," the stranger concluded.

I agreed to do this. It just so happened that the royalty checks from those cassette tapes replaced my total pastoral income—and then some.

I later found out that the man and his wife received the tapes after visiting our church for the first time. The woman liked a teaching called "Five Character-istics of a Happy Family," and the man liked "Seven Steps to Reaching Your Dreams." Then they sent the tapes to a publishing company on the east coast.

From that little connection, I more than doubled my income. The content on those tapes was ini-tially for a group of thirty adults. Through a divine connection, God amplified the teachings to 30,000 households! When you steward your season faithfully, you never know how God will use you. That's why the next chapter is about how to put on a posture of expectation.

ACTIVATE: Put On a Posture of Partnership

God uses divine connections to help the Body of Christ accomplish far more than any individual could on their own. A posture of partnership is critical to enjoying the fullness of God's favor!

The first step is choosing to partner with God. Consider the direction of your ambitions—are they oriented toward a kingdom purpose or fueled by visions of individual success?

Next, take stock of the people in your life. Oftentimes, we are only a few degrees of separation away from leaders in every domain of society. Where can you leverage the strengths of others? Who could you bless with your resources and knowledge?

Think about how this applies to business and financial spheres. When we have a kingdom focus, we don't care about getting the glory for ourselves. The collective mission transcends the individual brand, so we can reach wide to achieve a common good. However, when we seek first the kingdom, all will be added (see Matthew 6:33). Our brand benefits from God-directed partnerships as well.

CHAPTER 4

FAVOR FILLS A SPIRIT OF EXPECTATION

When you expect something to happen, you prepare for it.

Consider a couple who is eagerly awaiting their first baby. Before the mother's due date, the couple will make several visits to the doctor, enjoy a baby shower, and prepare a space for their newborn. Even if they are anxious about the new adventure at hand, joyful preparation overrides anxiety. They couldn't avoid having expectation even if they wanted to!

Joyful preparation overrides anxiety.

When you think about the future, what images pop into your head? Are your thoughts negative or positive? Perhaps you are afraid to think of anything at all because you don't want to risk disappointment. As people of faith, it is important to be aware of our expectations. Holy expectations align with God's Word and the promises He has given you.

One of my favorite biblical stories about expectation is in 2 Kings 3. To give you some context, the nation of Moab had just rebelled against Israel. So, King Joram of Israel and King Jehoshaphat of Judah joined forces to go into battle. However, after traveling for seven days in the wilderness, there ran out ofo water for the men and the animals. In desperation, they called for the prophet Elisha who was traveling with them.

Elisha asked for a harp player, presumably so he could worship and ask the Lord what He thought about the situation. As the harpist played, Elijah began to prophesy. As Elisha looked into the dry, desolate valley, he said,

Thus says the Lord: "Make this valley full of ditches." For thus says the Lord: "You shall not see wind, nor shall you see rain; yet that valley shall be filled with water, so that you, your cattle, and your animals may drink." And this is a simple matter in the sight of the Lord; He will also deliver the Moabites into your hand. Also you shall attack every fortified city and every choice city, and shall cut down every good tree, and stop up every spring of water, and ruin every good piece of land with stones (2 Kings 3:16-19 NKJV).

The ditches were not going to be filled by any natural phenomenon like rain or storms. Elisha prophesied that water would be provided by the Lord's power alone. What seems impossible to us is simple in the sight of the Lord. However, in order to receive the water, the people had to take a step of faith. God stirred up a spirit of expectation by asking the Israelites and Judeans to participate in the miracle. So they dug ditches and prayed that their efforts would result in water.

> *Now it happened in the morning, when the grain offering was offered, that suddenly water came by way of Edom, and the land was filled with water* (2 Kings 3:20 NKJV).

In response to their faithful digging, God's favor filled the ditches. The people's efforts were not in vain. Water was *everywhere.* And that was just the first miracle. The sun's reflection on the water gave it the appearance of blood. When the Moabites approached their camp, they thought Israel and Judah had slaughtered one another! They were sorely disappointed when they realized the optical illusion. Israel charged the Moabites and defeated them just as Elisha prophesied.

So not only did the water hydrate the Israelites, Judeans, and their livestock, it equipped them to defeat the Moabites in battle. Because they chose to align their expectations with the Word of God, God's favor fueled multiple miracles beyond what the people imagined. Holy expectations will help your faith grow, too. As you cultivate a posture of expectation, your faith will grow to such a height that it can reach the dreams God has stowed away in your treasure chest.

Give God a Vessel

The miracle of water filling the ditches affected matters on a national scale. Thousands of lives were spared in Israel and Judah, and many Moabite lives ended. The trajectory of those nations was altered forever.

The next chapter of 2 Kings reveals how God performs similar miracles on smaller scales. A recently widowed woman came to Elisha in her desperation. She told him that a creditor was going to enslave her sons if she didn't come up with some money fast. Here is what Elisha asked her to do:

> *Go outside, borrow vessels from all your neigh-*
> *bors, empty vessels and not too few. Then go in*
> *and shut the door behind yourself and your sons*

> *and pour into all these vessels. And when one is*
> *full, set it aside* (2 Kings 4:3-4 ESV).

So the widow obeyed and gathered several vessels. After she collected them, she began to pour oil, and her sons brought her the containers.

> *When the vessels were full, she said to her son, "Bring me another vessel." And he said to her, "There is not another." Then the oil stopped flowing. She came and told the man of God, and he said, "Go, sell the oil and pay your debts, and you and your sons can live on the rest"* (2 Kings 4:6-7 ESV).

Can you imagine the emotions the widow must have felt? First and foremost, there must have been an intense wave of gratitude and relief. Her family was supernaturally saved! However, after some time passed, I bet the widow thought to herself, *I should have gathered more vessels!* If she had, the oil would have continued to flow. With each container, more wealth would have been added to her. The widow had a degree of expectation because she reached out and listened to Elisha. However, this story shows us there is no limit when it comes to holy expectations.

In the Bible, oil is representative of the Holy Spirit. So the widow's testimony reveals a powerful truth about God's favor—the Holy Spirit will fill every single vessel you provide until it overflows. If we expectantly give God a space, He fills it.

Dig a Trench of Expectation

You may have heard the saying "Dress for the job you want, not the job you have." When I was younger, I took that adage to heart. I dressed in a coat and tie, went to work, and envisioned myself in the position I aspired to. In a way, that was digging a ditch of expectation.

As Christians, we must be intentional about where we direct our faith. Hebrews 11:1 (TPT) says, *"Now faith brings our hopes into reality and becomes the foundation needed to acquire the things we long for. It is all the evidence required to prove what is still unseen."* The images you see in your mind's eye reveal your hope. Hope is the framework faith attaches to. If you don't have faith for something unseen, you're not digging any trenches of expectation.

Romans 4:17 (ESV) says that God *"gives life to the dead and calls into existence things that do not exist."* There's a powerful principle here. We can use our words to direct our imaginations. When we speak our faith and declare truth over our lives, God can bring forth things that do not exist.

One of the greatest challenges in life is to align the chatter in your head with the Word of God. However, I've found that when I speak, my mind has to shut up and listen. For example, if you started to count from 1-10 in your head and then I asked you what your name was, what would happen? Your train of thought would be interrupted, and you'd stop counting to answer me.

 Speak scripture out loud to create an atmosphere of expectation that's rooted in God's promises.

What you say has more power than you think. Proverbs 18:12 says that life and death are in the power of the tongue. That's because words are never *just* words. As Jesus says in Luke 6:45, what you say flows from what is in your heart. Pay attention to how you speak to yourself and others. Then, declare the Word of God in private. As you speak scripture out loud, you will create an atmosphere of expectation that's rooted in God's promises.

Let Go

If you want God's favor to continually fill you, part of you must remain empty. There is a tension here. On one hand, we are to faithfully steward what God has entrusted to us in the current moment. On the other hand, we must remain connected to future hope and be ready to change as God directs. This requires leaving space in our days. When we fill our schedules in our own strength, we can suffocate what the Spirit wants to do in our lives. We can exchange miraculous multiplication for mundane management.

Living with a spirit of expectation requires you to relinquish control. The widow unwillingly let go of control—her husband died, and she was in a state of desperation. There wasn't much for her to control because she didn't have much.

Many times we don't ask God to fill us until we're depleted. Then we regain just enough strength for ourselves and (maybe) our families. But what would happen if we learned how to relinquish control willingly? Daily surrender would transform us into people who continually walk in God's favor. Generosity would flourish, and we would lavish blessings on others because we'd know we have more than enough.

You can exchange miraculous multiplication for mundane management by letting go of control.

What vessels are you surrendering, and which vessels are you holding too closely to the vest? When you invite the Holy Spirit into a space, it will be filled. Go ahead and dig the trenches. Look inside the cabinets and cupboards and start knocking on your neighbors' doors. Do whatever you must do to have a posture of expectation and watch God's favor fill the space!

ACTIVATE: Dig Ditches in Different Areas

Did you know that you can intentionally build your faith in different areas of your life? Perhaps you have faith that God will get you where you want to be in your career, but you struggle to believe He will come through in your relationships. So what do you do? Pray and ask God where to dig ditches. He may show you strategies, or there might be people along your path He nudges you to reach out to.

The same is true for your finances. People want financial favor, but they don't dig a ditch. How do you dig a ditch? By doing the hard work to gain financial knowledge and understanding. After you gain knowledge, it's time to get in the game and give God a vessel.

Financial vessels take many forms, including but not limited to: investments, businesses, nonprofits, real estate, your career, freelancing clients, etc.

Are there steps you can be taking to prepare the vessel so that when increase comes, you'll be ready? Whether it's a business plan, creating a budget, or employing a marketing strategy, consider how God might be inviting you to partner with Him in your current season. Favor follows surrender. Whenever we give a vessel to God, He will provide an increase.

ACTIVATE: Don't Despise the Day of Small Beginnings!

We've all been there. You're digging a trench, believing God for a miracle, but there's no water to be seen anywhere. When that's the case, keep digging! Seasons of preparation always come before seasons of provision. Don't despise your current season. It may look like a dry valley, but as you start believing God and letting the Holy Spirit speak into your life, you'll begin to see water. That's why Hebrews 11:1

(NKJV) says that *"faith is the substance of things hoped for, the evidence of things not seen."* To be a person of faith means to stay the course even when you don't see anything in the natural realm.

CHAPTER 5

FAVOR COMES BY REVELATION, NOT IMITATION

An orange sun bursting through a kaleidoscope of colors. Falling in love. Cradling your firstborn child in your arms. Diving into a piece of pecan pie or a slab of barbecued ribs fresh off the grill.

Each of these vignettes gives us a taste of something holy. Even those who don't claim to follow a religion feel something beyond themselves when they gaze at the ocean or embrace a loved one. Theologians refer to this concept as "general revelation." In some way or another, God has revealed Himself to all creation. Psalm 19:1-2 (NLT) has a beautiful way of describing general revelation:

The heavens proclaim the glory of God. The skies display his craftsmanship. Day after day they continue to speak; night after night they make him known.

God speaks to us in specific ways, too. Theologians call this "special revelation." As 1 Corinthians 2:12 (NLT) says, *"And we have received God's Spirit (not the world's spirit), so we can know the wonderful things God has freely given us."* Revelation is relational. It's a gift from God that proves His desire to have a relationship with us. God will confer favor in your life in personal ways. It will align with who He created you to be and the unique things you are designed to do. I like to say it this way: favor comes by revelation, not imitation. Matthew 16:13-18 (NLT) reveals that the source of all revelation is knowing that Jesus Christ is the Son of God:

When Jesus came to the region of Caesarea Philippi, he asked his disciples, "Who do people say that the Son of Man is?" "Well," they replied, "some say John the Baptist, some say

Elijah, and others say Jeremiah or one of the other prophets." Then he asked them, "But who do you say I am?" Simon Peter answered, "You are the Messiah, the Son of the living God." Jesus replied, "You are blessed, Simon son of John, because my Father in heaven has revealed this to you. You did not learn this from any human being. Now I say to you that you are Peter (which means 'rock'), *and upon this rock I will build my church, and all the powers of hell will not conquer it."*

Isn't it interesting that Jesus changed Simon's name to Peter after he received a divine revelation of His identity? We have the same tremendous privilege today—we get to hear from God! As the Body of Christ, revelation is the rock on which we are to build our lives. Divine insight from the Holy Spirit is how we fulfill our calling to build the Church and spread the gospel of the kingdom.

Beyond Imitation

Like Peter, we need revelation, not just knowledge from human beings. This doesn't meant that you shouldn't surround yourself with Christian role models and leaders. The issue becomes when you copy them because you think it's the only way to succeed.

Rather than listening to the Holy Spirit, taking steps of faith, and charting their own course, copycats try to play it safe by sticking to a proven method of success. This thought process propels people to get an MBA and enter the corporate world when God has really given them the desire to be a pastor. On the contrary, it's also the same thought process that propels people to become a pastor when God has really given them the desire to get an MBA and enter the corporate world. Somewhere along the way, they adopted a narrative of success and let that determine their direction rather than a revelation of God's will for their life.

In some respects, imitation is a natural part of the human experience. We spend the majority of our childhood echoing our parents and peers. We obtain good manners, habits, values, and even the ability to speak through imitation. However, as time passes, copying doesn't scratch the itch anymore. Kids start to test boundaries and ask "why" a thousand times a day. Eventually, there comes a need to make things personal. Information must become revelation. This is why Christians raised in the church notice a profound shift when they decide to make their faith their own. Perhaps it's also why, according to Barna Research, 64 percent of young adults with a Christian background are no longer involved in church.[9] Information about Christianity never took root as personal revelation.

Information must become personal revelation.

To receive new revelation, we often have to let go of old thinking patterns. As Jesus says in Mark 2:22, you don't put new wine into old wineskins. There will be multiple points throughout your life when God leads you new territory, whether it's a physical move, a career change, different relationships, or something else entirely. In some instances, you may have to physically change something to shake off to a any unhelpful mindsets adopted through imitation.

Consider Abram. God made him a grand promise, but before it could be fulfilled, Abram would have to leave his hometown of Heran. After his step of obedience, God says, *"Behold, my covenant is with you, and you shall be the father of a multitude of nations. No longer shall your name be called Abram, but Abraham, for I have made you the father of a multitude of nations"*)Genesis 17:4-5, ESV).

It was only after Abram took a leap of faith and left Heran that he received the revelation of who he was, not just what he could do. He became Abraham, the father of a multitude of nations. This probably sounded crazy to him—he still didn't have any children! Yet God prophetically called Abraham by who He created him to be, not how he saw himself.

Here's the thing—God's vision of who we are is much greater than how we view ourselves. Walking in God's favor daily requires a personal revelation of who you were created to be and what you are called to do. That's why imitation can be so toxic. It can cause you to compare and covet rather than delight in your destiny.

> **Imitation can cause you to compare and covet rather than delight in your destiny.**

Turn Aside and Look

Moses is one of the most revered people in the Bible. However, before he led the Israelites to the Promised Land, Moses spent several years sweating on the backside of the desert. In fact, the desert was his place of refuge after he murdered an Egyptian! (See Exodus 2:11-15.) When God first spoke to Moses, he was taking care of his father-in-law Jethro's flock in a town called Midian, which means strife. As he approached Mount Sinai, he saw something really strange:

> *And the Angel of the Lord appeared to him in a flame of fire the midst of a bush. So he looked, and behold, the bush was burning with fire, but the bush was not consumed. Then Moses said, "I will now turn aside and see this great sight, why the bush does not burn"* (Exodus 3:2-3 NKJV).

The desert was dry and hot, so it wasn't uncommon for a bush to catch on fire. What caught Moses's attention was the fact that the bush was not consumed. Whereas a standard plant would shrivel to a crisp, this one endured like a candle. Moses' decision to take notice of this anomaly made all the difference in the world.

> *So when the Lord saw that he turned aside to look, God called to him from the midst of the bush and said, "Moses, Moses!" And he said,*

"Here I am." Then He said, "Do not draw near this place. Take your sandals off your feet, for the place where you stand is holy ground" (Exodus 3:4-5 NKJV).

God didn't speak until Moses decided to turn and look. There are little fires beckoning you to pay attention to the presence of God. Similarly, the Holy Spirit is asking you, "Will you pause on your to-do list and consider what I'm doing today?"

If I am being honest, there are days when I don't feel like paying attention to God. That would involve stopping what I'm doing and diverting my path. Turning aside to look can be scary. There is no telling what God might ask us to surrender. Undoubtedly, it will require us to go beyond ourselves and serve. Consider the task Moses received as a reward for listening:

Look! The cry of the people of Israel has reached me, and I have seen how harshly the Egyptians abuse them. Now go, for I am sending you to

Pharaoh. You must lead my people Israel out of Egypt (Exodus 3:9-10 NLT).

Can you imagine how dumbfounded Moses must have been? In his mind, he was still a murderer destined to live out the rest of his days in the desert. Exodus 4:10 tells us that Moses wasn't a great orator, and he doubted his leadership potential. Yet he turned aside to look and was obedient anyway. Favor follows surrender. Once Moses gave his yes, God's grace covered the rest. From there, miracles far greater than a burning bush occurred. Enemies were defeated, and seas were parted. Do you want to experience the supernatural and live out who God created you to be? If so, you must be ready to divert your gaze and direction daily. That requires slowing down.

Favor follows surrender.

Pause and Listen

We live in a fast-paced culture. In the digital age of the twenty-first century, imitation has become even more continuous and covert. Constant internet access and pervasive social media compel us to mimic fashion choices, pick up trendy diets, or invest too much into financial fads because we fear missing out. For the most part, we can get what we want when we want it. DoorDash delivers our food demands, and most products are just a click away with Amazon.

If we're not careful, we can fall victim to a slew of false narratives:

- Instant gratification is better than waiting.
- More content equals more wisdom.
- Busyness is synonymous with productivity.

In fact, busyness is one of the quickest ways to kill progress. As author John Spencer writes, "Being busy is frantic while being productive is focused. Being busy is fueled by perfectionism while being productive is fueled by purpose."[10] As followers of Jesus, we measure productivity by transformation. We are concerned with becoming more like Christ and doing work that helps others do the same. Busyness can make it feel like we're moving forward. However, if we are not aligned with God's will for our lives, we are stagnant at best.

If we want to walk in God's favor, we cannot run at a pace that prevents us from listening. God typically doesn't speak to us with flashing lights or a booming voice from the sky. Usually, it's a still, small voice. Remember, burning bushes weren't that bizarre for a desert shepherd. If Moses had never seen one before, I bet he would've said something along the lines of, "Wow, that bush is on fire," not, "Why does the bush not burn?" The miraculous often comes through the ordinary. So, look for unusual signals in the mundane, from the carline at school to projects on your plate at work.

Luke 5:16 (AMP) reveals how Jesus lived at a pace that protected His connection to the presence of God. It says, *Jesus Himself would often slip away to the wilderness and pray [in seclusion]."* The Holy

Spirit is constantly trying to talk to you. There are burning bushes everywhere. However, like Jesus, we must slow down to notice them and prefer God's will to our own. Tunnel vision on our plans will confine our perspective to human limitations. However, surrender allows us to see the eternal, kingdom perspective God offers us.

Financial Revelation

We've all been there. The neighbor gets a brand-new car. That friend from college moves into a giant home. Your coworker just returned from an exotic vacation. Suddenly your truck feels inadequate, your house becomes stuffy, and you find yourself surveying flight prices in your spare time. Comparison leads to imitation, and financial imitation can diminish our bank accounts and spiritual health alike. We can find ourselves buying junk we don't need and focusing on the wrong things. Thankfully, God provides financial revelation specific to our situation when we ask.

Immediately after the burning bush revelation, God also gave Moses financial revelation. Exodus 3:21-22 (AMP) says,

> *And I will grant this people favor and respect in the sight of the Egyptians; therefore, it shall be that when you go, you will not go empty-handed. But every woman shall [insistently] ask her neighbor and any woman who lives in her house, for articles of silver and articles of gold, and clothing; and you shall put them on your sons and daughters. In this way you are to plunder the Egyptians [leaving bondage with great possessions that are rightfully yours].*

So when the time came, Moses instructed the Israelites to ask for the Egyptians' resources. Without the specific financial revelation God provided, they probably wouldn't have taken such a risk. The Israelites were being persecuted, after all. They were trying to leave the country fast! Instead, they applied God's wisdom, and it paid off big time:

Now the children of Israel had done according to the word of Moses, and they had asked from the Egyptians articles of silver, articles of gold, and clothing. And the Lord had given the people favor in the sight of the Egyptians, so that they granted them what they requested. Thus they plundered the Egyptians (Exodus 12:35-36 NKJV).

Thanks to financial revelation, the Israelites could move on to the next phase of their journey with ample provision. God will provide for all your needs, too. You do not have to work at a restless pace or copy others.

You don't need to imitate someone else's life to reach success.

Becky and I grew up in a small town, and opportunities felt few and far between. A spiritual mentor of ours used to encourage us by saying, "You can get anywhere in the world from the crossroads of highway 35 and 36." In other words, God can take you anywhere or bring you anyone from right where you are. You don't need to imitate someone else's life to reach success. To walk in God's favor, you must have your own revelation of what God has asked you to do.

Financial Seasons

If you don't listen to the Holy Spirit, it's amazing how many holes you'll have in your pockets. As you practice partnering with God in your finances, you'll become better at gauging the pace at which He wants you to grow. Your financial growth is connected to your spiritual growth. Like anything that grows, your finances will go through seasons. A significant part of financial revelation is discerning whether you are in spring, summer, fall, or winter.

 Your financial growth is connected to your spiritual growth.

Winter is a time of rest, listening, and what we call "hovering." Just as Genesis 1:2 recalls how the Spirit of God was "hovering over the face of the waters" before the creation of the universe, we must have quiet periods of perception and planning before we jump into something new. It's important to remain present in the winter. If you stay the course, you'll be ready to plant your vision when spring comes. After you plant your seeds, summer will approach quickly. Just as farmers must protect their crops from heat and pests in the hotter months, there will be a time when you must focus and ward off distractions in order to achieve your God-given goals. Finally, autumn is a time of collecting the harvest that your faithfulness has produced. This is a time to rejoice and give God the first fruits of your labor as you reap without complaint.

Without a revelation of your financial season, it's tempting to get antsy. You may plant something in the winter that would have grown better in the spring. Or you may try to harvest something that still has a long way to grow. Sometimes you will need to make decisions that set you back in the short term to position yourself for long-term growth.

In the long haul, you should be able to continually increase. Nonetheless, there will be prolonged winters when it seems like you're going backward or starting from scratch. Do your best not to get discouraged. Take a break, learn, and wait as God does a new thing inside you. Spring is always next. It happens every year.

ACTIVATE: Where Are You Tempted to Imitate?

Examine the big choices you've made throughout your life. Have they been made from a place of revelation or imitation? If the latter is true, it's never too late to get into the grace God has for your particular race. First, consider why you've imitated others—is there something about their lifestyle you desire? Is there a reason why you believe you should live a certain way? Sometimes we copy because there's something we want, and sometimes we copy because we feel like it's necessary to live a good and pleasing life.

Whether it's a want or a should, they both can turn into strongholds that keep you from receiving a revelation of God's will for your life. Diving into why you imitate a certain lifestyle or attitude will help you drill down to your core beliefs. Take a moment to process areas where you may be imitating—in your church, relationally, career-wise, financially, etc. Then pray and repent. On the other side is profound revelation of who God created you to be.

CHAPTER 6

FAVOR HAPPENS WHEN GOD LEADS

Have you ever prepared a surprise party for someone?

The week before the event is full of preparations. There are invitations to be sent, reservations to be made, and cake to be ordered. Soon enough, the day of the party comes and guests filter into the room. As the time approaches for the subject of honor to arrive, voices hush, lights dim, and anticipation builds. At the opportune moment, the door opens, and everyone yells, "Surprise!"

The birthday boy or girl has no idea that someone was working behind the scenes to prepare a space for them. God's favor works similarly in our lives. He constantly orchestrates people, places, and opportunities for our future. As Romans 8:28 (NLT) says, God causes everything to *"work together for the good of those who love God and are called according to his purpose for them."*

When God leads you to possess something, He will dispossess it beforehand and/or give you the strength to dispossess it yourself. To dispossess means to oust, evict, or remove. A key aspect of walking in God's favor involves learning to recognize the places God has emptied for you and then taking action to fill them. One of the most significant biblical examples of this is when God led the children of Israel to the Promised Land.

Long before God delivered the Israelites from slavery, He began divesting, or removing, the Egyptian army from the Promised Land. At the time, the Egyptian army was one of the most powerful militaries in the world. For centuries, they were spread throughout Canaan to control the land and keep people out of it.[11] However, 150 years before Joshua led the Israelites into the Promised Land, the Egyptian army began to leave. God used the reign of three different pharaohs to dispossess the land and prepare it for Israel's arrival. He also sent an angel before the Israelites to secure their success (see Exodus 23:23). Psalm 44:2-3 (AMPC) beautifully describes God's favor over the Israelites as they entered the Promised Land:

> *You drove out the nations with Your hand and it was Your power that gave [Israel] a home by rooting out the [heathen] peoples, but [Israel] You spread out. For they got not the land [of Canaan] in possession by their own sword, neither did their own arm save them; but Your right hand and Your arm and the light of Your countenance [did it], because You were favorable toward and did delight in them.*

God has been working on your behalf to clear a path for centuries, too. His favor will supernaturally equip you to enter areas that you could never reach in your own strength. As Joshua 24:13 (NKJV) says, *"I have given you a land for which you did not labor, and cities which you did not build, and you dwell in them; you eat of the vineyards and the olive groves which you did not plant.* "When the Israelites occupied the Promised Land, they didn't have to build a society from scratch. The pieces were already in place. God's grace went before them to prepare a home beyond what they could achieve.

I have heard countless stories from pastors about how God supernaturally provided a building for their church. My son, Brant, and daughter-in-law, Abi, are some of them. Their church outgrew their old space, so they searched for a new building. During that process, we encouraged them, "The Lord has a building for you. Just be patient. It will be the right space in the right location at the right time." Sure enough, a church moved out of a beautiful 35,000-square-foot building with its own parking lot (which is a big deal in Denver). The Lord supernaturally dispossessed the space and orchestrated the divine connections necessary to make it happen.

You might ask, "Well, of course God would do that for a church, but how does it apply to me?" If God does it for a pastor, He will do it for the Christian banker, politician, schoolteacher, and businessperson. Ephesians 4:4-7 (ESV) says:

> *There is one body and one Spirit—just as you were called to the one hope that belongs to your call—one Lord, one faith, one baptism, one God and Father of all, who is over all and through all and in all. But grace was given to each one of us according to the measure of Christ's gift.*

We all have a different measure of grace, or favor, for certain work. God's favor will prepare a place where you can be fruitful and multiply with the kingdom work you are equipped to do. He will lead you to the job, show you how to build the business, and give you the power to get the resources.

For example, we believe there is a mandate in our life to help people make sense of making money for making a difference. In other words, God gave us a passion for teaching people in the Body of Christ how to build wealth so they can use their resources to positively transform cities and nations. Throughout our lives, God has dispossessed areas that equipped us to fulfill our calling. As we've built our investment real estate portfolio, we have repeatedly witnessed God dispossess commercial and residential properties. By dispossessed, we don't mean that the properties were run down. Rather, we mean that God was intimately involved in the investment process. Not only did He guide us to the right properties, His favor coordinated the factors needed for the deals to transpire.

For example, one day we received a call from a banker out of the blue. He said, "I want you to go look at a property and tell me what you think about it." I went and assessed the land, and it truly was a valuable plot of dirt. So I called the banker back, and he said, "I'm going to sell you that land for what's owed on it." That amount was extremely below the market price, so it had to be divine intervention. We took the deal.

About three months later, I met the man who sold us the land. He said, "Billy, I want to thank you for doing me a favor." I was shocked—I had no idea what he was talking about! He continued, "If you hadn't bought that property when you did, I would have lost everything." That taught me a lesson. When God dispossesses something, it's usually a win-win.

Believe the Land Is Good

When we know there is a place prepared for us, it empowers us to move forward in confidence. God will clear the path, but a step of faith will always be required on our part. The Israelites approached that step with hesitancy. Before they entered the Promised Land, Moses sent spies to scope it out. They found so much abundance in Canaan that a single cluster of grapes had to be carried on a pole between two people. They reported, "*We came to the land to which you sent us. It flows with milk and honey, and this is its fruit. However, the people who dwell in the land are strong, and the cities are fortified and very large. And besides, we saw the descendants of Anak there"* (Num. 13:27-28 ESV).

God proves His faithfulness.

God repeatedly promised to give the Israelites the land, and He proved His faithfulness through miracle after miracle when they were in the wilderness. Still, they doubted. Even though the land was fruitful, the Israelites focused on their fear. The descendants of Anak were giants, after all! They didn't understand that God was leading them into what had been dispossessed, and it cost them greatly. Two men, Joshua and Caleb, were the only people who believed God would give them the Promised Land. Consequently, they were the only ones over the age of 20 God allowed to enter the land.

In Numbers 14:21-23 (ESV), God says, *"But truly, as I live, and as all the earth shall be filled with the glory of the Lord, none of the men who have seen my glory and my signs that I did in Egypt and in the wilderness, and yet have put me to the test these ten times and have not*

*obeyed my voice, shall see the land that I swore to give
to their fathers. And none of those who despised me shall
see it."*

Before you go too hard on the Israelites, remember that the only existence they had known was slavery and the desert. It must have been difficult for them to believe they could live in a land of freedom that was flowing with milk and honey! There will always be a chasm between your present reality and your hopes for the future. Are you believing God for something you've never experienced before?

Perhaps:

- ► Your parents had a poverty mindset, yet you want a life of abundance.

- ► You didn't grow up in a Christian home, but you long to leave a spiritual legacy for your children.

- ► The church has been a place of pain or even abuse in your life, yet you dream of being in a Christian community that reflects the kingdom of heaven.

➤ Everyone you know works a 9-5 job, but you feel like God is leading you to start a business or ministry.

When you become a Christian, God plants kingdom desires in your heart. These desires (and your faith for them to come to pass) might start small, but over time they will grow. As they do, mountains will move in your life and create space for others to experience the kingdom, too.

As Jesus says in Matthew 13:31-32 (NLT), *"The Kingdom of Heaven is like a mustard seed planted in a field. It is the smallest of all seeds, but it becomes the largest of garden plants; it grows into a tree, and birds come to make nests in its branches."*

It is essential to feed your faith even when God's promises seem impossible. Remember the thousands upon thousands of Israelites who could not enter the Promised Land because of their disbelief! The same holds true for us today. Trust that God is leading you into a land flowing with milk and honey and that He will give you the strength to defeat any giants that stand in your way.

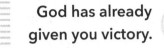 **God has already given you victory.**

Many times, Christians mistake resistance for the voice of the Holy Spirit. They say, "I don't have peace about that," and stay stuck where they are. Just because something is uncomfortable does not mean God is telling you not to do it. As you follow God, He will lead you to new frontiers that require deeper levels of faith. You are a pioneer for your family. It will require a fight if you want to break generational strongholds of poverty, sin, or fear. The good news is that God has already given you victory.

The Power of Patience

Whereas some people struggle with being too hesitant, others struggle with waiting for God's direction. They are trailblazers who fear missing out. Becky and I fit into this category. However, our prayer life changed once we had a revelation of how God's favor goes before us. We used to pray, "God, if it is Your will, please do x, y, and z." Now we pray for God to open our eyes to the opportunities and dispossessed areas around us. He's already working. If you believe that, it will help you exercise patience rather than hustling to make something happen yourself. The next season is coming—it's just not ready yet.

We all hurry and pick fruit before it is ripe from time to time. Waiting on God takes practice, and it often takes courage to obey Him. Ephesians 2:10 (ESV) says, *"For we are his workmanship, created in Christ Jesus for good works, which God prepared beforehand, that we should walk in them."* God prepared the good works, but we must choose to walk in them. In other words, be patient and trust God to ripen the fruit; but once it matures, don't hesitate to take a step of faith and pick it. If you wait for the timing of God in your life, you will continuously be astounded by the supernatural alignment of the environment He has prepared.

Becky and I have pursued the right thing at the wrong time, too. This doesn't always result in a major catastrophe. However, it feels like you're settling for less than God's best. It can also take the margin out of your schedule. It is easy to become so busy or preoccupied that you don't have the space to recognize the areas God has dispossessed for you—much less the bandwidth to enter them. If this happens to you frequently, take some time to identify the root cause. Why are you determined to blaze your own trail? Is there something you don't trust God will bring to fruition in your life?

When you wait for God to lead you into areas that have been dispossessed, He always takes you up a level. For example, we believe that God intentionally prepared our current home for us. It has everything we've dreamed of, right down to the finest detail. Our favorite place in the house is our back deck. It is drenched in peace and has a great view of the Colorado landscape and wildlife. We often sit there and reflect. We'll say to each other, "Can you believe that if that other contract went through or we acted in that timing, we'd be living somewhere else?" God's favor is just as present in closed doors as in open ones. It would not have fulfilled our desires if we had jumped the gun and bought a different house. It would have been fruit picked before its time.

How God Dispossesses Money

There is a chance this chapter has made you uncomfortable. Perhaps you're thinking, *Well, it's great that God dispossessed the Promised Land for the Israelites, but what about the Canaanites who lived there first?* When you think about your own life, it may be hard to stomach the idea of occupying an area at someone else's expense. If that's the case for you, it's important to remember that God is just. His favor in your life won't operate contrary to His character.

Deuteronomy 9:5 (NLT) reveals why God allowed Israel to occupy the Canaanites' land: *"It is not because you are so good or have such integrity that you are about to occupy their land. The Lord your God will drive these nations out ahead of you only because of their wickedness, and to fulfill the oath he swore to your ancestors Abraham, Isaac, and Jacob."*

The Canaanites had corrupt practices embedded into their culture. They worshipped demonic idols, partook in taboo sexual acts, and performed child sacrifices. So God dispossessed their property and gave His covenant people a chance to use it righteously. Theologian Andy Patton writes that this was "part of God's plan to cleanse the land of evil practices and push back the dark spiritual powers that had enslaved the people of Canaan."[12]

The land of Canaan was flowing with milk and honey. This wasn't just a pretty description. It indicated abundance. Milk meant plenty of livestock. Honey implied bees, revealing vegetation that needed to be pollinated. In an agrarian society where most people made their money from the land, the Israelites were rich.

God's will is for the righteous to prosper. However, today, immoral people still control much of the world's finances and make poor choices with their money. The good news is that this reality is temporary. Money is never static. Its value constantly fluctuates, and it is always changing hands. The Bible clarifies that wicked people won't keep their wealth forever. As Proverbs 13:22 (NKJV) says, *"A good man leaves an inheritance to his children's children, But the wealth of the sinner is stored up for the righteous."*

That begs the question: who are the righteous? For starters, righteous people use their resources for good, and wicked people use their resources for evil. In her book *Kingdom Calling,* Amy Sherman uses a quote by Reverend Tim Keller to describe a righteous person: "The righteous in the book of Proverbs are by definition those who are willing to disadvantage themselves for the community while the wicked are those who put their own economic, social, and personal needs ahead of the needs of the community."[13]

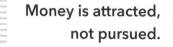

Money is attracted, not pursued.

So if you want God's favor to dispossess resources for you, pursue righteousness and steward what you have with integrity. Remember the Parable of the Talents (found in Matthew 25:14-20) that we mentioned in the first chapter? The servants who were given two and five talents doubled their investment in anticipation of their master's return.

However, the servant who was given one talent buried it in the ground. When the master returned, the servant dug it up and explained, *"Master, I knew you were a harsh man, harvesting crops you didn't plant and gathering crops you didn't cultivate. I was afraid I would lose your money, so I hid it in the earth"* (Matt. 25:24-25 NLT). Naturally, the master becomes angry. So he dispossesses the one talent from the unfaithful servant and hands it to the first servant, who has ten talents. He says, *"To those who use well what they are given, even more will be given, and they will have an abundance"* (Matt. 25:29 NLT). Money is attracted, not pursued. The one talent was attracted to the character of the servant with the ten. If you faithfully steward what you have been given, God will dispossess areas of abundance for you, too.

ACTIVATE: Reminisce on God's Faithfulness

Take time to reflect on how God's favor has opened and closed doors for you. What experiences, opportunities, or relationships have been pivotal in your life? Perhaps you didn't realize God was at work at the time. Reminiscing on God's faithfulness will build your faith and align your perspective for future opportunities.

God has a plan for your life, and His favor goes before you and behind you. Pray Isaiah 25:1 (NLT): *"O Lord, I will honor and praise your name, for you are my God. You do such wonderful things! You planned them long ago, and now you have accomplished them."*

Then ask God if there are any areas that He has dis-possessed for you in this season.

CHAPTER 7

FAVOR CULMINATES WHEN YOU ENTER YOUR LAND

What do you long for?

If you dig deep, I'm sure you will find dreams and desires God has placed in your heart. Perhaps you are hanging on to a promise He gave you long ago. In the last chapter, we discussed how generations of Israelites were in a similar situation. God promised them they would live in a land flowing with milk and honey despite years of slavery and wilderness wandering. Then God prepared the place and led them to it. All they had to do was obey and occupy. King David, described as a man after God's own heart, was one of the beneficiaries who lived and ruled in the Promised Land. In Psalm 16:5-6

(NLT), he writes, *"Lord, you alone are my inheritance, my cup of blessing. You guard all that is mine. The land you have given me is a pleasant land. What a wonderful inheritance!"*

King David knew that God would keep him safe in the land, and he was grateful for the inheritance he was given. Part of his inheritance was the land of Canaan. However, he had a spiritual legacy for following God as well. The same is true for us today. While we look forward to our ultimate inheritance in heaven, God has prepared a land for us in the here and now. Within the boundaries of your land there are people you are destined to meet, work you are meant to do, and places you will reach. The goal is to make the earthly kingdom look a little more like the heavenly kingdom so people can experience the goodness of God in the land of the living.

What Is Your Land?

Like the Israelites, there is a journey to get into your land. You must go through your own "Egypts" and overcome strongholds. There will be wilderness seasons when your faith is strengthened. All the while, God's favor equip you with specific gifts, talents, resources, connections, and experiences. Your land is the point of convergence where everything comes together to further the kingdom of heaven on earth. It's where the promise is fulfilled and the dream comes alive. In other words, your land is where the various displays of God's favor in your life converge.

> **Your land is where the various displays of God's favor in your life converge.**

In his acclaimed book *The Making of a Leader*, Dr. J. Robert Clinton describes convergence as a point in leadership development where a person's gift mix, experience, and temperament come together at a specific geographic location. He writes:

> In the long haul, God is preparing you for convergence. He is conforming you to the image of Christ (see Romans 8:28-29), and

He is giving you training and experience so that your gifts may be discovered. His goal is a Spirit-filled leader through whom the living Christ ministers, utilizing the leader's spiritual gifts.[14]

Convergence reminds Becky and me of one of our favorite Thanksgiving traditions. Before the meal, we purchase a new jigsaw puzzle. After everyone in our family is completely stuffed, we clear off the dining room table. Then we pass the time between seconds and dessert with a thousand-something-piece puzzle. Our excitement starts to build when we get to the last few pieces. Everyone wants to be the one to put in the final piece. That's what coming into your land feels like. All the nights you spent praying in faith for something you couldn't see yet start to make sense.

From Manna to the Land's Produce

Before the Israelites could enter the Promised Land, they had to undergo a period of spiritual maturation in the desert. There they learned how to hear, trust, and obey God's voice. Remember, generations of Israelites were forbidden to enter the land because they didn't believe that God would provide for them once they got there (see Numbers 14:21-23). After centuries of waiting and decades of wandering through the wilderness, Joshua 5:9-12 (MSG) describes the exciting evening before the Israelites entered the Promised Land. Here is what happened as they camped at the precipice of Canaan:

> God said to Joshua, "Today I have rolled away the reproach of Egypt." That's why the place is called The Gilgal. It's still called that.
>
> The People of Israel continued to camp at The Gilgal. They celebrated the Passover on the evening of the fourteenth day of the month on the plains of Jericho.
>
> Right away, the day after the Passover, they started eating the produce of that country, unraised bread and roasted grain. And then no more manna; the manna stopped. As soon as they started eating food grown in the land, there was

*no more manna for the People of Israel. That year
they ate from the crops of Canaan.*

As soon as the Israelites came into the Promised Land, the manna ceased. They ate a feast from the abundance of a land flowing with milk and honey! After generations of slavery and wilderness wandering, they had a place God gifted them as their own. Whereas manna was a miracle, there's no question that the favor the Israelites experienced in their own land was on a different level.

If you feel like you've been wandering for some time, unsure of God's will for your life, there is good news—the same God who led the Israelites into the Promised Land has a place for you, too. Favor culminates when you enter your land.

Break Your Manna Mindset

Before the Israelites could enter the Promised Land, they had to stop at Gilgal, which meant "roll away." There, God rolled away the reproach of Egypt. No longer would the Israelites view themselves as slaves. At Gilgal, God rolled away their old identity so they could claim their created purpose as His chosen people.

Part of that new identity entailed being landowners. Their entire livelihood was going to change. Before the Promised Land, God provided everything. He sent plagues to Egypt through Moses, parted the Red Sea so the Israelites could escape, and sent manna and quail from the sky. The Israelites simply followed and received, even when they had no idea what was going on. The word "manna" literally translates to: What is it?[15]

God's favor is woven into every area of your territory.

Fast-forward to "Canaan," which means merchant or trader.[16] In the Promised Land, things were going to be different. The Israelites would have a significant role in providing for themselves and their community. They lived in an agrarian society, which means most people worked as farmers. Unlike receiving manna, farming required a lot of intention, planning, and cultivating. This didn't make it any less miraculous. Only God can make seeds turn into crops that can sustain a nation! However, there was a higher degree of partnership on the Israelites' part. The Israelites put their hand to the plow, and God's favor gave them abundant harvests and success in the marketplace.

God wants to invite us into higher degrees of partnership, too. However, many Christians are still stuck in a manna mindset. They don't realize the degree of involvement God wants in their day-to-day endeavors, from their career to their finances. The Bible makes it clear that when you give, you will receive. However, people with a manna mindset think that the only way they will receive is when God drops favor on their head like ripe cherries off a tree. On the contrary, residents of the Promised Land recognize that God's favor is woven into every area of their territory.

Two Kinds of Money: Manna and Produce

There is still modern manna in our midst. Think about the timely financial miracles you've heard about or experienced. The money seemingly falls out of the sky—an unexplainable check arrives in the mailbox, a stranger pays it forward in the check-out line, a mission trip gets fully funded by donations, or a distant relative sends a gift. This money is transformational. It's given with the intent of transforming someone's life, not expecting anything in return from the recipient.

We experienced modern manna before our first daughter, Brooke, was born. In preparation for parenthood, Becky and I went to Lamaze classes. If you don't know, Lamaze classes provide breathing practice and exercises to help during childbirth. We attended those classes until it was finally time for Becky to give birth. Well, the classes might have equipped her, but they certainly didn't do anything for me! I passed out cold in the delivery room.

When I woke up, I found myself in the waiting room. As I was getting my bearings, a woman from our Lamaze class appeared. She pulled out a wrinkled $100 bill from her purse and said, "The Lord told me to give you this." As a new parent, that 100 bucks felt like a million dollars! It was a timely, supernatural blessing that met a real need.

Perhaps similar stories come to mind for you. This kind of receiving increases our faith and our desire to be generous. However, it's only the first step. What if we could receive a gift and immediately use it to serve others? Becky and I will never forget that $100. However, we'll also tell you this: it is way more fun to be on the side of giving the $100. As Acts 20:35 (NKJV) notes, Jesus Himself says, *"It is more blessed to give than to receive."*

 Look to the land, not the sky.

Modern manna is one of the first forms of financial involvement God has in our lives, but it was never meant to stop there. When you come into your land, the manna will cease. Instead, you will eat the produce of the land. The Israelites' income was dependent on their harvest. A fruitful land meant an abundant life. Today, few of us are farmers. So, the produce of the land signifies how we earn a living, whether it be via a job, business, or passive income investments.

Many people think that transformational money is the only financial involvement God will have in their life. They don't understand that He wants to show them favor on the transactional side as well. In other words, God will show you His favor in the land that He has for you. Sure, you may receive the occasional unexpected gift or check in the mail. However, when you partner with God in your land, you start to notice other things. It could be an unexpected increase in your commissions at work. It may be a new project that makes your creativity come alive. There could be favor with coworkers and superiors that brings peace to your workload. If you're a full-time investor or entrepreneur, perhaps it's an amazing opportunity to increase profits. We like to say it this way—look to the land, not the sky.

This isn't about becoming richer. New levels of provision come with new levels of partnership with God. Consider the Israelites. When they received manna, they didn't have to do too much. However, they couldn't really build anything or bless anyone with their resources, either. On the other hand, the Promised Land was abundant, but it came with work and a God-given assignment. With more blessing came more responsibility, and with more responsibility came more blessing. The Israelites were given special instructions to be generous with the fruitful land they were given.

For instance, God established gleaning laws that instructed the Israelites to leave extra crops from their harvest for the poor, orphans, and widows. Deuteronomy 24:19-21 (NLT) includes instructions for gleaning:

> *When you are harvesting your crops and forget to bring in a bundle of grain from your field,*

don't go back to get it. Leave it for the foreign-
ers, orphans, and widows. Then the Lord your
God will bless you in all you do. When you beat
the olives from your olive trees, don't go over
the boughs twice. Leave the remaining olives
for the foreigners, orphans, and widows. When
you gather the grapes in your vineyard, don't
glean the vines after they are picked. Leave the
remaining grapes for the foreigners, orphans,
and widows.

The countercultural kindness of Israel was intended to display the glory of their God to surrounding nations. In the new covenant, the Promised Land is not confined to a country. Jesus established the kingdom of heaven in its place, and its reign permeates throughout the entire earth.

Your land is your mission field. As you venture deeper into your Promised Land, there will be more abundance and blessing. However, it will require more of you, too. Whereas manna helps you survive, the produce of the land equips you to thrive. Can you imagine how powerful it would be if churches learned to receive transactionally? What if churches funded their operating costs from business revenue and investments? Then they could deploy the majority of the transformational money (tithes and offerings) to community outreach and kingdom building. To be clear, nonprofits can own assets and for-profit entities. You need a good accountant and a good lawyer, but it can be done. However, it's not common. More often than not, churches struggle to grow their finances in tandem with vision, and pastors are left without enough money to retire.

 God will provide fresh revelation of the work that needs to be done.

Whether you are a pastor or a pizza chef, every new horizon of your land comes with a new assignment. God will provide fresh revelation of the work that needs to be done. You will receive favor transactionally in your land as you pour out your time, talent, and resources. Unlike manna that only sustains you, these resources can be delegated to continue the kingdom work with which you have been entrusted. Being generous to others will richly bless you now and in heaven. This is what bringing heaven to earth looks like!

The Land's Endless Horizons

> *Do not be conformed to this world, but be transformed by the renewal of your mind, that by testing you may discern what is the will of God, what is good and acceptable and perfect* (Romans 12:2 ESV).

Coming into your land is really about coming into the will of God. You can do this in every season. Romans 12:2 tells us there is a good will of God, an acceptable will of God, and a perfect will of God, which don't contradict one another. Instead, this verse shows that being transformed by the renewal of our mind is a process. You aren't going to discern God's perfect will for a situation right off the bat.

The Greek word for "discern" is *dokimazō*,[17] and it often carries the sense of finding out the worth of something by putting it to the test. So we learn the will of God by renewing our minds to His Word *and* through trial and error. With each new horizon of our land, we are transformed to be more like Christ and to know God's perfect will more clearly.

As previously mentioned, you come into your land when you move from manna to produce. In other words, you cross over the threshold into your land when you shake the manna mindset and decide to use God's favor in your life to bless others. If you stay the course, it will ultimately lead you to your destiny. Jesus described this progression in Mark 4:26-29 (NKJV):

> *And He said, "The kingdom of God is as if a man should scatter seed on the ground, and should sleep by night and rise by day, and the seed should sprout and grow, he himself does not know how. For the earth yields crops by itself: first the blade, then the head, after that the full*

grain in the head. But when the grain ripens, immediately he puts in the sickle, because the harvest has come."

This parable dispelled familiar narratives about the Messiah's coming. Jews thought the Messiah, and consequently His kingdom, would come suddenly and all at once. On the contrary, Jesus revealed that it would come from small beginnings but with steady, astounding growth.

Life with Christ follows the same process. We often don't know how the Lord works in our lives. It is not a perfect parallel, but it's almost like the blade in the parable represents the *good will* of God, the head represents the *pleasing will* of God, and the full grain represents the *perfect will* of God. The point is that there is progressive growth; and one day, God reveals that the pieces are in place and there is a harvest to be collected in our land.

The highest form of favor is the honor of doing kingdom work in the place God has led you to. It is a reward for your patient and faithful obedience. As

Psalm 37:34 (NLT) says, *"Put your hope in the Lord. Travel steadily along his path. He will honor you by giving you the land. You will see the wicked destroyed."*

Coming Home

When you come into your land, it feels like coming home after a long journey. It's the satisfaction of finding what you've been looking for. There will be peace and presence in your work that's completely different from the striving you may have experienced in the past. No longer are you cursed by the sweat of your brow, but you are fruitful and multiplying in the land as God originally intended. It's like everything you have lived for and learned has culminated into one place.

As long as you live, you will move from glory to glory (see 2 Corinthians 3:18). However, it doesn't stop there. As good as the Promised Land is, it's still only a shadow of the kingdom to come. The ultimate horizon of our land—*"the holy city, the new Jerusalem, coming down from God out of heaven like a bride beautifully dressed for her husband"*—described in Revelation 21:2 (NLT) is still ahead of us.

May God open your eyes to the favorable land He has prepared for you. May you have the strength to remain faithful to the journey until we are together in the kingdom of heaven!

ACTIVATE: Roll Away the Reproach

Have you already had your Gilgal moment? Or are there mindsets that need to change before you can walk into your Promised Land? It would be great if we could just take our minds out and scrub them with a brush and some soap. Pain, shame, and a whole host of other things can build up in our brains if we don't renew our minds to the Word of God like Romans 12:2 encourages.

Favor becomes a part of you when you roll away any mentality that contradicts your identity as a child of God. Believe that God has a land flowing with milk and honey for you and dare to dream big about the possibilities. Meditate on Psalm 37:3-4 (NLT):

"*Trust in the Lord and do good. Then you will live safely in the land and prosper. Take delight in the Lord, and he will give you your heart's desires.*"

NOTES

1. Genesis 6:5-6.
2. Walk; Strong's H1980; https://www.blueletterbible.org/lexicon/h1980/nlt/wlc/0-8/#lexResults; accessed February 15, 2023.
3. Grace, Favor; Strong's G5485; https://www.blueletterbible.org/lexicon/g5485/kjv/tr/0-1/; accessed February 15, 2023.
4. Jehoiachin; https://www.biblestudytools.com/dictionaries/hitchcocks-bible-names/jehoiachin.html; accessed February 15, 2023.
5. Fred Dunkley, Safehaven, "Nearly One-Third of U.S. Lottery Winners Declare Bankruptcy," *Wolf Street*, April 17, 2018; https://wolfstreet.com/2018/04/17/nearly-one-third-of-u-s-lottery-winners-declare-bankruptcy/; accessed February 15, 2023.
6. cf. Genesis 12:4 with Genesis 21:5.
7. Erin Urban, "What Is Your Impact?" *Forbes*, October 16, 2017; https://www.forbes.com/sites/

forbescoachescouncil/2017/10/16/what-is-your
-impact/?sh=7811c43e6f35; accessed February 15,
2023.

8. McKinley Valentine, "Chronos vs Kairos:
    Understanding how the Ancient Greeks viewed time
    will make your life richer," *The Whippet*, 9 March 2020;
    https://thewhippet.org/unsolicited-advice/kairos/;
    accessed February 15, 2023.

9. "Church Dropouts Have Risen to 64%—But What
    About Those Who Stay?" *Barna Group*, September
    4, 2019; https://www.barna.com/research/resilient
    -disciples/; accessed February 15, 2023.

10. John Spencer, "The Difference Between Being
    Busy and Being Productive," June 26, 2018; https://
    spencerauthor.com/rest/; accessed February 15, 2023.

11. Estera Wieja, "From Moses to Jesus: Egypt in
    the Bible and Today," *Fellowship of Israel Related
    Ministries*, March 31, 2021; https://firmisrael.org/
    learn/from-moses-to-jesus-egypt-in-the-bible-and
    -today-2/#:~:text=We%20know%20from%20the%
    20Bible,prosperous%20nation%20in%20the%20
    region; accessed February 15, 2023.

12. Andy Patton, "Why Did God Command the Invasion
    of Canaan in the Book of Joshua?" BibleProject.com,
    2021; https://bibleproject.com/blog/why-did-god

-command-the-invasion-of-canaan-in-the-book-of
-joshua/; accessed February 16, 2023.

13. Amy L. Sherman, *Kingdom Calling: Vocational Stewardship for the Common Good* (Downer's Grove, IL: InterVarsity Press, 2011), 87.

14. Robert Clinton, *The Making of a Leader: Recognizing the Lessons and Stages of Leadership Development* (Carol Stream, IL: NavPress, 2012).

15. Manna; Strong's H4478; https://www.blueletterbible .org/lexicon/h4478/kjv/wlc/0-1/; accessed February 16, 2023.

16. Canaan; Strong's H3667; https://www.blueletterbible .org/lexicon/h3667/kjv/wlc/0-1/; accessed February 16, 2023.

17. Discern; Strong's G1381; SermonIndex.net; https:// www.sermonindex.net/modules/articles/index .php?view=article&aid=34682; accessed February 16, 2023.

ABOUT THE AUTHORS

Billy and Becky Epperhart have been married 48 years and have dedicated their time to doing business and ministry together. They have founded several organizations, including WealthBuilders, Tricord Global, and WealthBuilders Investments. In addition, Billy is the CEO of Andrew Wommack Ministries and Charis Bible College, as well as the co-director of Charis Business School. Billy and Becky share a collective passion to teach others how to make sense of making money for making a difference. When they aren't leading, teaching, or preaching, the Epperharts love to spend time traveling the world and being with their four grandsons.